ASCD | arias

ASSESSING MULTILINGUAL LEARNERS

A Month-by-Month Guide

Margo **GOTTLIEB**

ASCD

Alexandria, VA USA

ASCD | arias

Website: www.ascd.org   www.ascdarias.org
E-mail: books@ascd.org

Copyright © 2017 by ASCD. All rights reserved. It is illegal to reproduce copies of this work in print or electronic format (including reproductions displayed on a secure intranet or stored in a retrieval system or other electronic storage device from which copies can be made or displayed) without the prior written permission of the publisher. Readers who wish to duplicate material copyrighted by ASCD may do so for a small fee by contacting the Copyright Clearance Center (CCC), 222 Rosewood Dr., Danvers, MA 01923, USA (phone: 978-750-8400; fax: 978-646-8600; Web: www.copyright.com). To inquire about site licensing options or any other reuse, contact ASCD Permissions at www.ascd.org/permissions, permissions@ascd.org, or 703-575-5749. Send translation inquiries to translations@ascd.org.

Printed in the United States of America. ASCD publications present a variety of viewpoints. The views expressed or implied in this book should not be interpreted as official positions of the Association.

ASCD®, ASCD LEARN TEACH LEAD®, ASCD ARIAS®, and ANSWERS YOU NEED FROM VOICES YOU TRUST® are trademarks owned by ASCD and may not be used without permission. All other referenced trademarks are the property of their respective owners.

PAPERBACK ISBN: 978-1-4166-2450-9   ASCD product #SF117076

Also available as an e-book (see Books in Print for the ISBNs).

Library of Congress Cataloging-in-Publication Data

Names: Gottlieb, Margo, author.
Title: Assessing multilingual learners : a month-by-month guide / by Margo Gottlieb.
Description: Alexandria, Virginia : ASCD, [2017] | Includes bibliographical references.
Identifiers: LCCN 2017014772 | ISBN 9781416624509 (pbk.)
Subjects: LCSH: Multilingual education. | Multilingualism in children. | Language arts--Ability testing.
Classification: LCC LC3715 .G67 2017 | DDC 404/.2083--dc23 LC record available at https://lccn.loc.gov/2017014772

25 24 23 22 21 20 19 18 17   1 2 3 4 5 6 7 8 9 10

ASCD | arias

ASSESSING MULTILINGUAL LEARNERS

A
Month-by-Month Guide

Want to earn a free ASCD Arias e-book?
Your opinion counts! Please take 2–3 minutes to give
us your feedback on this publication. All survey
respondents will be entered into a drawing to
win an ASCD Arias e-book.

Please visit
www.ascd.org/ariasfeedback

Thank you!

Introduction

This is the story of Ana, a newcomer to the United States and the American school system. As we unveil each month, you will witness how assessment affects students, teachers, families, and school leaders at Lincoln Elementary School. It reveals how a school implementing dual-language education seeks to balance the types of measures, the languages of assessment, and the uses of data for decision making. In doing so, Lincoln, in moving toward distributed assessment leadership, seeks to instill agency in students, empower its teachers, and engage families.

Ana, a diminutive, pony-tailed seven-year-old, timidly walks into her new school, gently holding her mother's hand. Excited about making friends and anxious to show her teacher that she already knows how to read and write, she manages a faint smile as she walks into the office. Today is Ana's first day at Lincoln, a mid-sized school serving grades K–8 that, with its budding multilingual student population, could fit any demographic—urban, suburban, or rural—in the country.

Ana is a bit apprehensive, as she doesn't understand what the person behind the counter is saying. The secretary then gestures to two chairs for Ana and her mother to sit. Soon another woman appears and reaches out to the two saying, 'Hola. Bienvenidas.' The two-word greeting—hello and welcome—spoken in Spanish, the home language of Ana and her mother, that put mother and daughter at ease could have been spoken in any of the myriad of other languages of the school's student population.

Lincoln School has had an influx of newcomers from war-torn countries over the past couple of years, many of whom have ventured up from Central America to join the community's growing, yet stable, Hispanic community. A schoolwide professional learning community of teachers and school leaders has been formed in preparation for integrating its students with interrupted formal education (SIFE) from around the world with students born and raised in the United States. The group's immediate task is to create an assessment timeline to capture the students' baseline data and to determine their subsequent growth throughout the school year. One of the major considerations is to ensure a balanced representation of the students' languages of instruction in assessment. Accountability for learning at the state level has historically only been in English and Lincoln, as well as the other schools in the district, is determined to counter that policy by providing strong evidence of student accomplishment in two languages.

August, September, October

August

The first couple of hours are a whirlwind of activity for Ana. It is registration time at Lincoln for the upcoming school year and rectangular folding tables have been set up all over the gym. A bilingual paraprofessional who serves as the school's community liaison escorts Ana and her mother to a table that has a looming sign above that says 'Screening.' First, they complete some paperwork that includes demographic, health, and education information. Fortunately, the paraprofessional has remained with Ana and her mother throughout the process; she now asks Ana's mother the remaining questions on the language-use survey, a statewide tool used to identify the potential pool of ELs, in Spanish:

1. Which languages do you and your family members use at home? ¿Cuáles son los idiomas que usan ustedes en casa con la familia?

2. Which languages does your child speak? ¿Cuáles son los idiomas que habla su hija?

3. Which languages does your child understand? ¿Cuáles son los idiomas que entienden su hijo/a?

The purpose of this initial **screening** is to determine whether students are exposed to and use languages other than English in daily interaction with family members. If any of the answers to this short language-use survey indicate daily contact with other languages, students then take a standardized English language proficiency screening test to determine whether they meet the criteria for ELs and qualify for language support. The Every Student Succeeds Act (ESSA), the 2015 reauthorization of the 1965 Elementary and Secondary Education Act, requires that each state create a uniform process for identifying ELs, provide language services, document the progress of ELs, reclassify students when they meet the requisite criteria, and monitor students post reclassification for up to four years.

As Ana is a newcomer to a U.S. school, screening in English requires less time than the 90 minutes that have been allotted. Additionally, as part of the district's enrollment process, writing samples in the student's home language are collected. Ana happily responds to the question written in Spanish for primary grade students: 'Describe tu animal favorito con detalles. Después dibújalo.' (Describe your favorite animal, with details. Then draw a picture of it). She proudly produces a short narrative and illustration of her dog, Pecas, who she misses dearly.

Results of Initial Screening. The results from these multiple measures—the demographic data, the survey questions, the screening test, and the writing sample—indicate that Ana qualifies to participate in the school's language education program. Here is a synopsis of Ana's results from the initial screening:

- Is the student from a home where languages other than English are spoken? *Yes*
- Has the student had continuity of educational experiences? If so, where? *Yes, in Mexico*
- What is the student's levels of English-language proficiency on a 6-point scale (with 5.0 considered English proficient) based on the screener?
  — Listening: *2*
  — Speaking: *1*
  — Reading: *1*
  — Writing: *1*
  — Overall composite: *1.5*
- Is there evidence of literacy in the student's home language? *Yes*

Knowing that Ana has had continuity of educational experiences starting in preschool, has attended school regularly, and can produce a story in Spanish makes her the ideal candidate to prosper in two languages—and Lincoln has several options for students like Ana to do so. Ana will be able to continue her education in Spanish while simultaneously be exposed to grade-level language and content in English.

Placement Decisions. The information gleaned from the initial screening helps determine Ana's classroom placement. Ana's mother listens very carefully to the choices and decides that the dual-language program—which enables Ana to continue to further her academic Spanish development while simultaneously accruing knowledge and understanding of

English through content-area instruction—would be ideal for her daughter. In the dual-language classroom, Spanish-speaking English learners (ELs) and proficient English speakers, some of whom are heritage-language speakers and former ELs, sit side-by-side as instruction is delivered in two languages throughout the day.

The following is a summary of the placement decisions for Ana based on the initial screening phase of assessment:

- Which grade level for the student? *2nd grade*
- Is the student eligibility for English-language support? *Yes*
- Is the student to continue her home language and literacy development? *Yes*
- Which programmatic option has been selected? *The dual-language program in English and Spanish*

The community liaison walks Ana to her classroom, where she is greeted by a smiling teacher who bends over and says to her newest student...¡Qué lindo que estés en nuestra clase! (How nice that you are in our class!).

September

Ana's placement in a 2nd grade dual-language classroom where instruction and assessment are delivered in two languages exemplifies the growing trend of this instructional design across the nation. The surge of enrollment in dual-language education has been prompted by legislation, most recently the passage of Proposition 58 in California, the growing body of literature and research from multiple fields (neuroscience, cognitive science, economics, linguistics, and language education, to name a few) that boosts the benefits of bilingualism, efficacy studies, program evaluations that substantiate its positive effects, and passionate advocates.

As it's the beginning of the school year, classroom teachers in Lincoln School are dedicating this month to the collection of baseline data on students' initial performance in the content areas as well as their language and literacy development. Luisa, Ana's teacher, sets up a chart to capture the data that she gathers on her students and then transfers the information to a software program that she and other teachers maintain throughout the academic year. Later, during collaboration time, she will discuss the overall performance of her classroom with her grade-level team.

Luisa, an experienced dual-language teacher, makes sure that she always relies on multiple sources of data for decision making. For some content areas, such as language arts, Luisa uses measures—such as Informal Reading Inventories in Spanish and English, **diagnostic tools** designed to ascertain students' frustration, instructional, and independent reading levels—agreed upon by her grade-level team. She notes data on the students' word recognition and comprehension on an Excel spreadsheet that is shared gradewide to document the reading progress of all dual-language 2nd graders in the same way and in the same place in both languages. These **pre-post measures**, selected by the dual-language instructional coaches and participating teachers, are administered again in May (the close of the academic year) to determine individual student growth in biliteracy development.

One way in which Luisa documents individual students' gains throughout the year is by making **anecdotal notes** of their conceptual knowledge in the content areas in conjunction with their academic language development. The evidence she collects is from the students' everyday instructional activities. Figure 1 shows Luisa's notes for Ana. (Luisa tries to complete a chart for each student every month and often jots down pivotal moments based on observation or interaction with the students.) You can see how Luisa capitalizes on Ana's strength in Spanish as a springboard for her English language development. As science is taught in English and social studies in Spanish, Luisa makes notations in the corresponding cells.

As second graders are not yet well versed in taking surveys, Luisa takes time throughout the month to interview individual students to get to know each one better. This year, Luisa has designed an **interest survey** to find out her students' passions, experiences, preferences, and even their dislikes. In that way, she can personalize instruction to motivate and engage her students to maximize their opportunities to learn.

Today, at the close of the **interview**, taking all her baseline data into account, Luisa sits down with Ana. Together they recap the first several weeks of school and decide on personal language goals in English and Spanish for the marking period. Knowing that Ana has strong literacy skills in

FIGURE 1: **Gathering Baseline Data Across the Content Areas**

Name: Ana   Month: September

	In English	In Spanish
Language Development	Transfers meaning from Spanish to English	Recounts personal narratives with much detail
Mathematics	Calculates raw addition to 1,000	Uses manipulatives in base 10
Science	Classifies physical properties of real-life materials	
Social Studies		Collects interview data on the community

Spanish, her teacher reinforces that strength in Ana's additional language, English. Here are the goals on which the two agree:

- *Language goal for English*: Label everything you see in our room. Ask your friends to help you.
- *Language goal for Spanish*: Look for what's similar in reading Spanish and English. In your journal, list words, phrases, and even short sentences that look alike and mean the same in the two languages—in other words, cognates.

Luisa's professional learning community of K–2 teachers has been studying theory, research, and practice related to the advantages of bilingualism and their impact on learning. Consequently, she is quite aware of the literature that points to the benefit of Spanish-speaking students' use of cognate knowledge to infer meaning in English. In this case, Luisa believes that since Ana's literacy in Spanish is very strong, she can readily and intentionally transfer information from one language to another, thus increasing her metalinguistic awareness. Having this strategic tool (that is, use of cognate knowledge) will be advantageous for Ana as it will enable her to gain a richer understanding of language use in her biliteracy development. As building cognate knowledge has been set as a language goal for Spanish for Ana and other multilingual students this initial quarter, Luisa notes that it should also be incorporated into the assessment repertoire of the classroom.

October

The second graders are very excited about Halloween and El Día de los Muertos (Day of the Dead), so Luisa and her teacher team have been busy crafting a multidisciplinary unit that integrates the content areas of language arts, mathematics, and social science with art, music, and language development. The teachers adhere to a methodology that includes a gradual release of responsibility so that the students begin to exhibit self-regulation and independent learning. As they wish to give the students choice and voice, the team decides to share with their classes a menu of three projects to be completed during the last two weeks of the month. Students are to work in pairs to:

- Construct a three-dimensional (3-D) mask from illustrated directions, describe it in detail, and explain step-by-step how it is made;
- Construct an ofrenda (an offering) for Day of the Dead from illustrated directions, describe it in detail, and explain step-by-step how to put it together; or
- Construct a 3-D map of the community from illustrated directions, describe a Trick or Treat route step-by-step, and explain in detail why you decided to go that way.

Since Ana is familiar with the Day of the Dead and has seen ofrendas in Mexico, she selects this project—which will give her an opportunity to explore her ancestry and her cultural roots. Ultimately she can share her language and culture with her partner, create an ofrenda that is significant for her and the members of her close-knit family, and start to make comparisons with the American holiday.

Ana chooses to combine video, a new technology for her (which she learns from her partner), audio storytelling about her ancestry (from information she has gathered through interviews with her family), and a written description of how she puts together the ofrenda. While Ana decides on Spanish as her primary mode of communication, she carefully labels the pieces of her ofrenda with brief descriptions in English to show she is beginning to communicate in her new language.

This **common performance assessment** for this month's 2nd grade project consists of the product each student has chosen, the agreed-upon criteria for success, and each student's personal reflections. It's considered common assessment as all 2nd grade teachers have reached consensus on the project's two-week time span, its three final products, and its associated rubric based on the criteria for success used to interpret student work. The overall purpose of this project is to determine the extent to which the students:

- demonstrate understanding of cross-cultural traditions,
- follow illustrated directions to create an original product, and
- explain the process of 'how' or tell 'why' they constructed or used their product either orally, through video, and/or in writing with illustrations.

This multidisciplinary project spans several content areas. The teachers rely on multiple sets of grade-level content standards for language arts, mathematics, science, and social studies as well as corresponding language development standards, including:

- Challenging academic content standards for English language arts for all students
- Common core en español for Spanish language arts for multilingual learners
- Next Generation Science Standards for all students
- C3 framework for social studies for all students
- WIDA English language development standards for the ELs
- WIDA Spanish language development standards for the multilingual learners

The second grade teacher team is committed to having students actively explore, experiment, and engage in learning. Therefore, the teachers rely on performance assessment in their instructional routines (in which students work with partners or in small groups) as well as for the culminating projects for each unit of learning. They realize that the students, as they work together and participate in academic conversations, are developing critical 21st century skills, are engaging in social interaction, and are being exposed to a variety of language models.

Performance Assessment. As Lincoln's teachers are committed to having students actively involved in their own learning, they craft each unit's products or projects (often with input from their students) that serve as the basis for performance assessment. Following is the list of specific features of performance assessment that Lincoln's teachers treat as their ongoing design checklist at grade-level meetings:

Performance Assessment—

☐ Represents students' identities, languages, and cultures

☐ Consists of authentic tasks with real-life application, ideally that take on social action

☐ Requires hands-on student engagement, preferably in collaboration with peers

☐ Exemplifies original student work that includes multiple modalities

☐ Is built from features of universal design for learning

☐ Connects to students' lives, interests, and experiences

☐ Offers evidence for learning based on standards-referenced criteria for success

Student evidence for learning is embedded in the teaching cycle throughout the two-week period (which may be extended, depending on the depth and breadth of the theme). Guided by their teacher, students have opportunities to self-reflect on their progress in their journals. Ultimately students decide which artifacts of their projects, including explanatory videos, descriptive written samples, and photos are worthy of being placed in their portfolios along with justifications for their selections.

Criteria for Success in Project-Based Assessment. Performance assessment of students' original work on their projects is interpreted using grade-level common rubrics with a series of descriptors that serve as criteria for success. For the dual-language classrooms, the teams of teachers and data coaches from each grade design oral and written analytic scales in English and Spanish that cover students' conceptual and language development. The rubrics have components that align vertically from grade to grade for all students, and that for ELs scaffold horizontally from one level of language proficiency to the next.

Dedicated time is allocated for the 2nd grade team to meet to co-create and discuss the descriptors for the project-based rubric. This month the students have a choice of presenting explanations for their projects either orally or in writing, in either English or Spanish, along with their exhibit. The team identifies a common set of criteria across modes and languages for the students, who are categorized as Beginners, Intermediate, or Advanced dual-language learners.

Their project rubric consists of criteria related to both language development and achievement, but today the team is focusing on language development. Together the teachers adapt grades 2–3 *Can Do Descriptors, Key Uses* (WIDA, 2016) and *los descriptores Podemos* (WIDA, 2016) in conjunction with the language development standards' Performance Definitions as starting points. They take individual descriptors related to productive language—speaking and writing—and convert them into a developmental five-point scale.

As all the projects require students to either describe in detail the 'how' or 'why' of a process, the team crafts criteria for success associated with explanations. The following is a sampling of agreed-upon criteria descriptive of oral and written language development in English and Spanish for the 2nd grade project for multilingual students at each language proficiency level. To show various ways of organizing criteria for two languages, the sample oral criteria are translations of one another while those for written language offer two complementary criteria.

Sample Criteria for Oral Explanations

Beginners Level (Nivel emergente):

- Express steps from illustrations of processes.
- Expresar pasos de procesos ilustrados.

Beginners + Level (Nivel emergente +):

- Describe steps with some details from illustrations of processes.
- Describir pasos de procesos ilustrados con unos detalles.

Intermediate Level (Nivel de desarrollo):

- Present ideas of content-area processes using sequential language.
- Presentar ideas de procesos académicos usando lenguaje secuencial.

Intermediate + Level (Nivel de desarrollo +):
- Present ideas related to content-area processes or procedures step by step using sequential language.
- Presentar ideas relacionadas de procesos o procedimientos académicos paso a paso usando lenguaje secuencial.

Advanced Level (Nivel de tranformación):
- Connect detailed ideas in content-related processes or procedures.
- Conectar ideas detalladas en procesos o procedimientos académicos.

Sample Criteria for Written Explanations

Beginners Level (Nivel emergente):
- Label broad elements or steps of processes or procedures from models.
- Explicar unos pasos de proceses o procedimientos usando palabras, frases modelo, e ilustraciones.

Beginners + Level (Nivel emergente +):
- Label elements or steps of processes or procedures from model sentences.
- Explicar unos pasos de procesos o procedimientos usando unas oraciones modelo e ilustraciones.

Intermediate Level (Nivel de desarrollo):
- Describe elements or steps of processes or procedures.
- Explicar los pasos de procesos o procedimientos con definiciones usando gráficas e illustraciones.

Intermediate + Level (Nivel de desarrollo +):
- Describe elements or steps of content-related processes or procedures.
- Explicar los pasos de procesos o procedimientos con definiciones y unos detalles usando gráficas e illustraciones.

Advanced Level (Nivel de tranformación):
- Express connected ideas descriptive of elements or steps related to content-related processes or procedures.
- Explicar los pasos con detalles describiendo el 'cómo' o el 'porqué' de procesos o procedimientos.

As Luisa wants to ensure that all her students understand the expectations for the project, which includes the oral or written explanation and the exhibit, she spends some time with her class translating the criteria for explanations in the grade-specific rubric into student-friendly language. In addition, she converts the criteria into a checklist for her students which, with its two options, is developmentally appropriate for second graders. Luisa introduces the notion of **student self-assessment** early in the school year, and believes that this project is a concrete example of how every student can determine whether or not their display and explanation have met the specific criteria.

With the criteria presented in two languages, Ana is excited to participate in determining the extent to which she has met the project's targets—something she wasn't able to do in her other school. Ana enthusiastically delves into the

checklist, which, as part of the common assessment, con-
tains criteria similar to those used by the 2nd grade teachers
when they come together to score the projects.

Inter-Rater Reliability. Having settled on the criteria for
success specified in the rubric and having collected the students' final projects after the schoolwide exhibition, the
2nd grade team must now determine their inter-rater reliability—that is, the extent to which the teachers agree on the
assignment of language proficiency levels for the projects.
Establishing inter-rater agreement ensures the maintenance
of consistency in scoring of all teachers and instills confidence that students would receive the same score in any of
the 2nd grade classrooms. The higher the reliability (generally 85 percent agreement or greater) in exact and adjacent
scores on the five-point scale, the greater the assurance of
accuracy in the results. As the principal of Lincoln School
relies on grade-level common assessment as part of the
school's local accountability for its dual-language program, it
is important to keep track of this statistic project by project.

The project rubric serves as a criterion-referenced scoring guide. In this case, the teachers match the criteria for
explanations to those that the students produce in their projects. They then assign beginners, beginners +, intermediate,
intermediate +, or advanced language development levels to
2nd graders other than their own. At the beginning of the
year, the teachers double-score each student sample to vali-
date their inter-rater agreement; later they only double-score
when there are discrepancies by more than one level. Ana's

language development for the project proves to be at the beginners level in English and the advanced level in Spanish.

◇◇

First Quarter Summary of Assessment and Its Extension to Other School Contexts

At the close of each quarter, we are stepping back and taking some time to revisit the most salient assessment tools that have been described and generalize their usability to all ELs. Often there is wide-range applicability of these assessment principles and practices to the general education community as well. We hope that you see opportunities to collaborate with other teachers or can work in grade-level teams to co-plan, implement, and co-interpret assessment results.

Screening, Identification, and Placement of English Learners

ESSA stipulates that state education agencies (SEAs) that receive Title III grants are to consult with local educational agencies (LEAs) to design and implement "standardized, statewide entrance and exit procedures" for ELs. As a result, all students new to a school district are required to respond to several state-level questions in order to make an initial determination: are the students from home backgrounds where languages other than English are spoken in daily inter-action? If so, these students are then ushered through a screening process. The purpose of this first round of testing is to identify ELs who then qualify for language support.

To the extent feasible, all students who have home lan-guages other than English, whether ELs or not, should have opportunities to show their full range of oral language and literacy development. To that end, as part of the screening process, school districts should consider collecting informa-tion on students' interests, language(s) of interaction with others, and writing sample(s). As literacy is a known predic-tor of achievement, teachers should make every attempt to ascertain the extent to which students can communicate in English and other languages.

Diagnosing Students' Strengths and Challenges

At the start of any school year, teachers must take time to get to know every one of their students. By ascertaining their students' skills and conceptual attainment across the content areas, teachers are better able to group students, plan instruction, and scaffold their learning experiences. For multilingual learners, teachers must also consider the stu-dents' levels of English language proficiency, including their receptive (listening and reading) and productive (speak-ing and writing) skills. These baseline data often serve as a touchpoint for comparison throughout the school year.

Diagnosing ELs' strengths and challenges can be accomplished in multiple ways. For example, content and language may be totally integrated for instruction and classroom assessment, yet when it comes time to interpret the data, students' academic language use is teased from their conceptual understanding. A language-centered approach might involve investigating the extent to which students are familiar with the features of grade-level genres (or text types) and how those differ from one content area to the next. A content-based approach, on the other hand, might rely on more traditional diagnostic measures that zero in on specific content-based knowledge and skills.

Taking Anecdotal Notes

With technology such as computers, hand-held devices, and mobile phones so easily available these days, teachers can readily catalog their instructional activities and record student responses. For example, teachers (or the students themselves) can tally student-student interactions based on specific purposes, document students' pivotal (aha) understandings and convert them into teachable moments, and tape student responses to open-ended questions.

Anecdotal notes should be dated and provide specific information about student performance along with the context of the learning experience. Information collected over time can serve as additional evidence for requesting specialized services (for example, for ELs who have been traumatized who could benefit from social work, for ELs who potentially have learning disabilities, or for ELs who are gifted and talented).

Embarking on Common Performance Assessment

Performance assessment should be integral to teachers' instructional routines; as an extension, common assessment should be performance-based and represent a body of work for a particular content topic or theme at the culmination of a period of study. Common performance assessment, as exemplified in a curricular framework that centers on backward design (Wiggins & McTighe, 2005), provides the impetus for teachers in grade-level teams to co-plan and come to agreement on the essential questions for a unit of learning and how to measure them. In turn, students are encouraged to express the desired results in authentic ways and transfer their learning to new situations.

Another curricular framework designed specifically for ELs highlights academic language use within content learning and incorporates assessment within and across lessons (Gottlieb & Ernst Slavit, 2014). In this framework, ELs and other learners are actively involved in meaningful activities including projects and presentations that peak their interest, foster language development alongside conceptual development, and reflect learning through performance assessment.

Introducing Student Self-Assessment

The sooner students can begin to take control of their own learning, the better. Students, including ELs, long-term ELs, ELs with disabilities, and students with interrupted formal education (SIFE) should contribute to and become familiar with the criteria of success used to evaluate the quality of their work. The criteria, coupled with exemplars at each performance level and practice, give students ample means to judge their accomplishments in relation to agreed-upon expectations. (Note: when working with ELs, it is important for teachers to allow for multimodal pathways to success that are sensitive to and reflective of the students' levels of English language proficiency.)

November, December, January

November

It's the close of the first quarter, which is marked by student-led conferences that are based on **portfolio assessment**. Since the beginning of the year, students have been carefully collecting artifacts of their learning; some of the entries are required for all students and include project descriptors, while others are selected by the students. Time has been devoted to having students organize their creative pieces and their artifacts, craft a Table of Contents, write an introductory welcome letter to their families, and produce an overall summary of their entries along with their personal reactions.

Once their portfolios have been arranged, students have opportunities to practice asking and answering questions with their peers about their work. Luisa makes time to meet individually with Ana and everyone else in her class; she carefully listens to Ana rehearse before the big night. She encourages the students, dispels their fears, and offers them concrete feedback on the kinds of questions to ask as well as ways to display and describe the contents of their portfolios.

Knowing that her mother plans to come for portfolio night, Ana writes the introduction to her portfolio in Spanish. She can't wait to share all that she has accomplished in Spanish while she has been learning English. While portfolio night invites family members to become part of the school community, Lincoln School goes beyond this traditional approach to family engagement. The school seeks to understand families' cultural and language practices (for example, by encouraging the capturing of oral story telling in their home languages as a schoolwide genre). Ana's ofrenda project, whose photographic artifacts populate her portfolio, exemplifies how families are integral to connecting home life to student learning.

Reading Response Logs as Assessment Tools. During portfolio night, Ana shows her mother her language arts' **reading response log**, which she has stored in her special folder. Ana has made tremendous strides in reading since her arrival in August. She has kept a list of the predictable-patterned books that she has already tackled in English along with the more advanced chapter books in Spanish. When she completes each book, Ana jots down the title and author, illustrates her thoughts in English, adds some newly acquired labels and phrases, and carefully crafts a synopsis and personal reflection for each entry in Spanish. Luisa, who makes anecdotal notes on each student's biliteracy progress on a monthly basis, offers comments and feedback to Ana.

Ana is lucky that her classroom is filled with informational and narrative texts that correspond to 2nd grade curricular themes in addition to selections from many Spanish-speaking countries. As well, digital resources are bookmarked in the classroom's computers and personal devices for students who wish to experiment with technology and advance their digital literacy. During portfolio night, Ana takes pride in choosing one of her favorite stories from the bookshelf and sharing it in a read-aloud with her mother.

Luisa has carefully filled the classroom library with an array of books and other resources reflecting the interests of her students and the range of their literacy levels in Spanish and English. Other considerations important in selecting books that are 'just right' for display include their linguistic and cultural relevance, the connection of the themes to the students' lives, and whether the message encourages students to take social action. Luisa's preference is that the literature in her room represents Hispanic authors and illustrators rather than translations of books written in English. Among the books are those in which there is a strategic presence of both Spanish and English; in other words, the pages are filled with examples of translanguaging.

Translanguaging and Assessment. Translanguaging is a means by which multilingual students make meaning by accessing more than one language, thus maximizing their communication potential with others who share their languages. Ana is comforted by books that contain translanguaging as she is able to glean the gist of illustrated stories in English, recognize the Spanish words that are sprinkled throughout and use them as context clues, and feel good about seeing her home language in print alongside English. One of the basic tenets of translanguaging is the assumption that multilinguals have one linguistic reservoir in which they can flexibly use all their linguistic resources to make sense of their world.

This year, Luisa has been experimenting with translanguaging as a pedagogical practice. She realizes that through the complementary use of two languages, multilingual learners can more readily rely on their full linguistic repertoire rather than be restricted by a single language. She has seen how Ana and others have thrived in this classroom ecology by being able to engage in academic conversations and deeply discuss text with partners and in small groups. Translanguaging, increasingly being adopted as a policy in schools with multilingual learners, has gained legitimacy as a pedagogy and a home-language practice.

If translanguaging is indeed interwoven into instruction, it axiomatically becomes part of assessment. In dual-language classrooms such as Ana's where the teacher is well versed in multiple languages, the use of translanguaging is a valid means of assessing multilingual students' content-based concepts and skills. When assessment is confined to one language (as has historically been the practice) and ELs are not proficient in that language, their true academic achievement is masked. However, when teachers and students share languages, assessment of content knowledge can be relatively independent of the students' language proficiency. Allowing students to demonstrate what they know using the language capital at their disposal in multimodal ways gives educators a better measure of their actual content-area performance.

Ana's translanguaging practices differ greatly from those of her classmates. In fact, multilinguals engage in unique patterns of language use based on their language proficiency levels in two or more languages and the language proficiencies of the persons with whom they interact. Therefore, the use of translanguaging in assessment is highly personalized and should be confined to the interactions of each student with their peers and teachers. As the presence of this phenomenon is highly individualized, so should its documentation. Ultimately, translanguaging that occurs between students, whether in academic conversations or written text, should be considered **assessment *as* learning** where students themselves have agency in demonstrating what they know, take responsibility for learning, and share it with others (Gottlieb, 2016). Teachers' trusting of students' language choices within supportive dual-language environments yields positive social, emotional, and academic results.

Read-Alouds as Personalized Assessment for Building Metalinguistic and Metacognitive Awareness. Luisa is thinking about how she can document Ana's and the other students' metacognitive and metalinguistic awareness, the

Spanish language goal for this quarter, within the context of literacy. She decides to use teacher **read-alouds** from illustrated books in Spanish as this strategy simultaneously invites students to participate in the reading process and supports their language development. In read-alouds, teachers model reading, thinking, and linguistic behaviors that help students develop schema and expectations for different types of text. Students interact with their teachers to discover language connections (metalinguistic awareness) and text/conceptual connections (metacognitive awareness). Later, the experiences are extended by having students engage in rich discussions with their peers.

Ana, as do other students, enjoys analyzing text in Spanish read-alouds and thinking about what it means. For each line of the short poem about a mosquito, students create a follow-up question to ask their classmates. Ana formulates the following questions (translated here) in Spanish: Why do you think that there is only one mosquito?; Where did all the mosquitos go?; I wonder, where is the mosquito's mother?; and What is the mother doing if she isn't with her baby?

The students form small groups to come up with the answers and then exchange their responses with one another. All the while, Luisa is taking notes on each student's ability to ask and answer questions, which is directly tied to grade-level language arts standards. The read-aloud strategy has given Luisa a great deal of insight into Ana's and her classmates' metacognitive awareness.

Un solo mosquito (A lone mosquito)
No hay ningún más. (There aren't any more.)
¿ Qué pasó con su mamita?
(What happened to its mother?)
¡Se quedó para atrás! (She's left behind!)

Another strategy Luisa is contemplating introducing to further the students' metalinguistic awareness is the notion of cognates. Cognates are words in one language that correspond in both meaning and form to words in another language. In this short poem, 'mosquito' is a cognate as it is identical in Spanish and English. So for Ana, by knowing the word in Spanish she automatically acquires a new word in English! Also, 'mamita' is a diminutive word of affection for 'mamá,' a recognizable word in text for most second graders. Luisa plans to take advantage of this similarity in languages to find out the different names her students have for their mother (assuming all students live with their mothers) and generate a list of synonyms. Even though all of her ELs speak Spanish, they represent many Latino cultures—including Mexican, Puerto Rican, Central American, and South American. Once students gain familiarity with cognates, Luisa expects that they will apply this metalinguistic strategy, which in and of itself might be considered a form of translanguaging, to individualized assessment and instruction.

December

In October, common assessment of a 2nd grade project using an agreed-upon rubric constructed by the grade-level team was highlighted. In December, as throughout the year, Luisa also focuses her attention on instructional assessment that occurs only in her classroom. Data are collected during instruction, where evidence as and for learning is embedded within classroom activities within the teaching cycle. As instructional assessment generates data for formative purposes, such as revisiting and improving teaching in the moment, many teachers choose to use the term 'formative assessment' (my personal preference, however, is **assessment** *for* **learning** to emphasize its intent and use of data for both teachers and students).

The purpose of instructional assessment is to mark some aspect of student performance that occurs day-by-day and to offer specific feedback, based on a lesson's objectives, that pushes student learning forward. For Ana and other students in dual-language settings, this translates into thinking about how to measure and offer criterion-referenced feedback in English and Spanish. Luisa is careful to balance her comments about her students' work in both languages so they are perceived as having equal status.

At times, the grade-level rubrics used for projects are deconstructed for instructional assessment in individual classrooms. The idiosyncratic application of a common rubric by different teachers and their students makes sense as each classroom is unique in its sociocultural make up and teaching-learning context, yet committed to achieving the same learning targets. In this way, instructional assessment across the grade is anchored in criteria that have been derived from the same data sources. Luisa often divides her students into the three groups as designated in the project-based rubric—Beginners, Intermediate, and Advanced—that she uses as the basis for scaffolding instruction and meeting the language needs of each student.

Some teachers incorporate the descriptors from the grade-level rubric into learning objectives that are shared with students. Others have students more actively engage in determining what the descriptors mean and the nature of the evidence they plan to attach to demonstrate their learning. Luisa chooses to break down the K–2 rubric for explanations with her students to design differentiated objectives that apply to English and Spanish for her different groups of students. Afterwards, she designs a checklist with her students. As they engage in learning, the students are prompted to use the checklist to help guide how to proceed in their assignments or activities.

Criterion-Referenced Feedback. A key feature of instructional assessment is timely feedback, criterion-referenced information that flows from teacher to student, student to teacher, or student to student. In most cases, the criteria are derived from standards, but can also include classroom norms, character building or social emotional learning, use of technology, and expectations for fine or performing arts. In providing feedback on their project requiring explanations, for example, Luisa might say to a student pair, "You followed the first step of the directions. Now look closely at steps 2 and 3. Show me the evidence that you followed these steps. What do you need to do next?" She prefers guiding students by providing them with concrete actions to take rather than using traditional grading practices and finds that students are more motivated when feedback is personalized, meaningful, and provides specific information.

Observation as an Instructional Assessment Strategy. Sometimes instructional assessment is spontaneous rather than planned, such as when teachable moments for Luisa spark the transfer of conceptual understanding from one language to the other for her students. As we witnessed in November, dual-language teachers are always intent in finding ways to build students' metalinguistic and metacognitive awareness within and across languages. In these instances, there are not necessarily any predetermined rubrics or checklists in hand. **Anecdotal notes** from everyday observations are the most authentic way to capture individual student performance. Luisa, who keeps a notebook with a page dedicated to each student, often places a colored Post-it on a student's page as a way of recording a pivotal moment in a student's understanding. During student observation, Luisa interacts with Ana and others as she believes that by providing concrete, actionable feedback, she gives her students opportunities to move toward self-regulated, independent learning.

January

It's a new calendar year and it's hard to believe that Lincoln School is approaching the close of the first semester. Students are now familiar with common performance assessment and can lead, with guidance from their teachers, in the identification of criteria for success for extended tasks and projects. In addition, they are comfortable with instructional routines, readily exchange information with their peers in academic conversations, and realize that assessment is always interwoven into the fabric of classroom instruction.

Ana and her classmates have been nurtured by a caring teacher who has provided a supportive and safe environment for experimenting and learning. As a result, students take risks and are gradually becoming empowered, have increased confidence, and exhibit agency. This educational philosophy and these instructional assessment strategies were not familiar to Ana, whose first-grade experience was traditional and teacher-centered with limited planned interaction among students. Gradually, Ana has become more engaged in learning with her peers in pairs and in small groups.

One way in which this 2nd grade class has grown emotionally and academically is through **self- and peer assessment**. The expectations that the students agree upon for projects, such as those shown in Figure 2, can easily be converted into a checklist. Luisa introduces checklists early in the school year with the students and now she feels that they ready to apply the criteria to their own work and that

FIGURE 2: **Checklist of Criteria for Project Success**

Names: _____ and _____

Our Project: _____   Date: _____

What We Can Do	What We Did
1. Follow directions.	
2. Create a story or a report.	
3. Show what we learned.	
4. Explain each step.	
5. Describe our project in detail.	

of their classmates. The generic checklist (see Figure 2) for student pairs can easily be expressed as a project-specific narrative, or another column could be added for students to show how each criterion has been met.

◇◇

Second Quarter Summary of Assessment and Its Application to Other School Contexts

It's hard to believe that we have already reached the mid-year point in the school calendar. Teachers and students have become well versed in instructional and assessment routines. Together they are synchronized in teaching and learning procedures and processes. Teachers are gradually moving students toward self-regulation; students are taking responsibility for setting goals for learning and providing evidence of meeting their goals. The assessment tools high-lighted this quarter center on how students are acting as learners who are more independent thinkers.

Organizing Portfolio Assessment

Portfolios have historically served as collections of student work that represent academic performance over time; when ELs are involved, however, portfolios should also show-case language development. Ideally, portfolio assessment is a learner-centered approach for documenting growth in which students have opportunities to collect evidence, select entries, and reflect on their learning.

In Ana's case, we see how portfolios can serve as the focal point of student-led conferences and the focus of conversations with family members. Portfolio assessment, depending on its ultimate purpose, can be implemented at multiple levels—from students to classrooms to grades or departments to schools. One of the hallmarks of portfolio assessment is that there is a uniform set of criteria, often in the form of a rubric, that is reliably applied to individual samples and to the portfolio as a whole. In that way, results can be aggregated and contribute to local accountability.

Maintaining Learning Logs

Learning logs are a unique record of student reasoning, learning, and reacting tied to one or more content areas. Often, students are invited to use these logs as a venue for recounting scientific procedures, explaining mathematical processes, or arguing in favor of or against specific social science issues. For ELs, learning logs offer non-judgmental space for sharing their attitudes toward their new language and culture. For these students and others, logs may also serve as a means of expressing their innermost thoughts and emotions.

Reading response logs are a form of learning logs appropriate for language arts; interactive journals, which reveal students' reactions to their overall learning experiences, are another. Knowing that there are broad parameters of expression with these logs, students have freedom to wonder and pose questions. Learning logs, including reading response logs, and interactive journals are forms of personalized assessment and, as they are individualized and confidential, should never be graded. Teachers are welcome to pose some guiding questions and respond with notes of interest to extend and deepen student thinking, with ownership residing with the students.

Embracing Instructional Assessment

When assessment is ingrained in the instructional routine, teachers are continually measuring student learning (as are the students) and improving their pedagogical practices based on ongoing data. Instructional assessment, by being classroom-based, is managed by each teacher in collaboration with her students. The feedback that teachers give students is geared to the content expectations of the learning activity and additionally, for ELs, for their academic language use in relation to their levels of language proficiency.

Instructional assessment generally operates on a lesson-by-lesson basis. For ELs, teachers must be in tune to the interplay of language and content to be able to differentiate and personalize instruction and assessment accordingly. As instructional assessment is ideally tied to classroom conditions that optimize and maintain student learning, teachers must be acutely aware of student characteristics. In classrooms with ELs, classroom conditions must include connections and accessibility to grade-level content, sensitivity to the students' multimodal uses of language, and the acknowledgment of multiliteracies as expressions of communication. Instruction, in tandem with assessment, should challenge students cognitively as well as linguistically within their zones of proximal development (Vgotsky, 1978).

Extending Self- and Peer Assessment

During this quarter, students are gradually given more autonomy in learning and assessment choices. Learning logs can be considered student self-assessment that promote metacognition and, for ELs, they also build metalinguistic awareness. The same holds true for read-alouds. Although teacher-modeled throughout the year, students can gradually take turns with this activity with partners or rotate their participation in small groups. The notion of self-reflection can be extended to having students design checklists or other forms of documentation based on lesson objectives and standards that have been converted to student-friendly language.

Peer assessment should proceed when students are familiar with the norms and procedures for self-assessment and feel confident offering evidence for their classmate's performance. It is another vehicle for empowering students as they assume agency in making judgments and defend their decisions to others. When students agree on the same criteria as the anchor for their work in a naturally occurring context, then 21st century skills of collaboration and cooperation are sure to follow. Outside of dual-language and bilingual contexts, EL student work is most likely produced in English; there is no reason, however, that when it comes time for peer assessment and students' home languages are shared, discussion or clarification of their work during peer assessment cannot be conducted in their home language.

◇◇

February, March, April

February

At the beginning of this second semester, the school seems to go into high gear in preparation for state testing. First is **English language proficiency (ELP) testing**, the state accountability measure for ELs in grades K–12. The test covers four language domains—reading, writing, listening, and speaking; districts generally can administer it online or with paper and pencil. Under ESSA, schools must build English proficiency attainment and growth rates into their accountability framework for Title I—the major funding source that supports low-income students.

The English-language proficiency test is more comprehensive than the screener given to Ana upon her entry in Lincoln School. The test provides scale scores that can be compared from year-to-year; these scores are converted into language proficiency levels for the language domains for literacy—reading and writing—and for oral language—listening and speaking—as well as an overall composite score. In Ana's case, score reports are generated for families that depict individual student results graphically, for teachers that show how their class performed, for schools by grade, and for districts for each school. Being sensitive to the many multilingual families in the state, the family report has been translated into their representative languages.

Ana's district has decided to administer the online version of the English language proficiency test. Before the actual testing window opens, teachers immerse themselves in the online training materials, attend webinars, become familiar with the test administration manual, and take a test to certify their qualifications. The technology coordinator at Lincoln School figures out the logistics and schedule for moving the students in and out of the computer facility. She also makes sure that there are enough earphones and that the computers have enough bandwidth to ensure the efficient transfer of data.

As many 2nd graders, including Ana, have not had opportunities to become acclimated to using computers for assessment, instruction, or personal entertainment, time is devoted to practice runs to familiarize students with the elements on the computer screen, how to advance using arrows, and how to record their voices. Ana feels simultaneously a bit intimidated and nervous but ready to take on the challenge. An advantage of computer-generated assessment (and instruction) over paper and pencil formats is that it can readily incorporate video, animation, and other multimodalities that stimulate student engagement and foster accessibility to the test content.

Using Multiple Modalities in Assessment and Instruction. During instructional time, Luisa has noticed that her students exhibit an extensive range of biliteracy development. With so many different performance levels, Luisa has been compelled to explore more non-traditional venues for her students to make meaning while simultaneously engaging them in higher-order thinking. She and other teachers have come to rely on multiple modalities, appealing to different senses, as a routine classroom strategy for assessment and instruction. When grade-level teams at Lincoln School come together, they brainstorm ideas as to how students can express what they are learning verbally, visually, and musically (such as through multimedia, video, or other technologies in addition to text).

The acceptance and use of multiple modalities for both instruction and assessment seems to have positively influenced the literacy development of Lincoln School's students—increasing interest, motivation, and engagement in learning. As the teachers and school leaders come to embrace this strategy, they realize that multiple modalities encompass whatever means students choose to communicate or enhance communication. For ELs such as Ana, having additional legitimate ways to express themselves, including their language of choice, has led to more confident, energetic learners.

March

This month, Lincoln School, as are all schools in the state, is devoting time to preparation and administration of **achievement tests in reading/English language arts and mathematics** for federal accountability for students in grades three through eight. Lincoln School also follows the state mandate for science testing, which occurs in grades 4 and 7. There is a designated two-week window during which all testing must be completed and the school is abuzz with figuring out the logistics and a timetable. The results of these **high-stakes state tests**, which determine the annual ranking of schools, are published in a state-issued report card each fall.

Lincoln School's teacher teams have crafted an aligned K–8 curriculum grounded in challenging state academic content standards that anchor these annual state measures used for **summative purposes**. With special consideration for ELs, ELs with disabilities, and students with interrupted formal education (SIFE), they have carefully connected content standards with language development standards to create complementary pairs. For dual-language classrooms such as Luisa's, the teachers have taken the extra step of adding Spanish language arts standards to the mix and have matched them to corresponding Spanish language development standards. Even though representative teachers and school leaders have previously selected an annual Spanish achievement test, they feel that more district-level data are necessary; they break into small groups to investigate various interim measures.

Interim Assessment. As a 2nd grader, Ana is not yet included in state achievement testing. However, in preparation for the upcoming year, she and her classmates as the remaining upper grades participate in **interim assessment**. A committee of teachers representing each school in the district has selected a commercially published test for reading/English language arts and mathematics. Administered in October and March, these measures are intended to have predictive validity; in essence, they serve as practice tests for the high-stakes state tests. Although Ana, as she is a newcomer to English, is exempt this year from the district's large-scale interim English language arts testing, she must take the mathematics test.

The state has recently transitioned from paper and pencil testing to an online format, so the district replicates the conditions for testing. There are additional considerations for ELs and ELs with disabilities (such as, for example, those students with minimal familiarity with keyboarding, as is Ana's situation). Fortunately, there is a set of accessibility and accommodation guidelines for the interim district tests that mirror those of the state.

Issues of Validity in Assessment of Multilingual Learners. When dealing with **standardized achievement tests**, whether administered on an interim or annual basis, teachers and school leaders should be concerned with their validity. It is always important to know that these commercially produced tests indeed measure what they purport to measure and that they are fair representations of what the test takers can do. One of the criteria that deems the inferences from standardized tests valid is the extent of demographic match between the norming population and the students who take the tests and are directly impacted by the results. High-stakes measures, such as the ones designated for statewide account-ability, can potentially yield grave consequences for individual students, schools, or districts. Therefore, to the extent feasible, bias should be minimized and validity maximized.

The pool of biases, which potentially reduces the validity of tests, are plentiful for Title 1 students. Linguistic, cultural, economic, religious, and national origin factors all impact the development of tests, their administration, and the results. Additionally, bias is readily introduced if ELs and ELs with disabilities are not included throughout the test development process, including cognitive labs, pilot testing, and field testing.

Research indicates that the results of ELs' achievement testing, when conducted in English, do not provide valid inferences about the students' content-area knowledge. In large part this is attributed to the fact that there is unnecessary linguistic complexity in the items that confound content area outcomes. Therefore, for a more accurate portrait of student performance, it is critical that accountability in dual-language programs rests on measures both in English and the home language of ELs. Consider Ana, although she clearly has the content knowledge, as evidenced by classroom assessment in Spanish, she is definitely a beginner in her English-language development. Taking any achievement test in English would not be a valid indicator of Ana's true conceptual knowledge and indeed a frustrating experience for this young girl.

Language Proficiency Testing v. Academic Achievement Testing. As Ana is one of many ELs in Lincoln School, it is important that the faculty understands the relationship between language proficiency and achievement. Luisa and the other teachers at Lincoln School have been involved in a year-long study of how to leverage language in curriculum design. Teacher teams have taken grade-level themes in English and Spanish that had previously been aligned to challenging state academic standards and embedded key uses of academic language. By creating a seamless integrated curriculum with rigorous content paired with academic language use, teachers find that although language proficiency and academic achievement are indeed different constructs, they tend to reinforce and strengthen each other. Thus, when everyday instructional assessment gives way to annual state testing, ELs, as all students, have the language to tackle content and the content to understand language.

April

As Ana is participating in the dual-language program, besides collecting data from common assessment in the students' preferred language, the school is committed to elevating the status of learning in Spanish. Therefore, the principal, having conferred with her staff, feels that administering a **standardized achievement test in Spanish** for local accountability purposes every other year, starting in grade two, is necessary for program evaluation and to have concrete evidence that students are making academic gains. The community, teachers, and the principal of Lincoln School hold a series of meetings. Together they strategically decide that standardized testing begin with Spanish to redouble the school's commitment to dual-language education. The school leadership, though aware of the downside of testing young students, feels that as long as the testing is a valid gauge of students' progress, it is a worthwhile endeavor.

Lincoln School's principal is aware that she needs a confluence of data from multiple sources that are both quantitative (such as the standardized tools) and qualitative (including the classroom portfolios) to demonstrate to families, the community at large, and the Board of Education that the dual-language program indeed benefits both ELs and proficient English speakers. To highlight the school's mission, vision, and accomplishments, the principal, along with teachers and students, prepare for the annual school fair at the end of the month.

The school fair is a celebration of the accomplishments of the year. Here, bilingual data are highlighted in grade-level posters and a school video captures the daily school life of multilingual learners. There are running monitors of students speaking about their interests and experiences and projects in multiple languages. Original student work fills every nook and cranny of classrooms and halls. Each classroom has selected a type of performance—re-enactments, musicals, one-act plays, recitations, dramatizations, to name a few—to create and present at the fair—which boasts multicultural exhibits, decorations, and treats.

Third Quarter Summary of Assessment and Its Application to Other School Contexts

This quarter is devoted to ensuring students become accustomed to large-scale testing formats and procedures. As many states are now testing online, students must become familiar with how test items are virtually delivered and how responses are recorded. Additionally, given the federal regulations for ESSA, many states and districts are in transition from one test to another and one testing mode to another. State and district testing plans will help stakeholders understand the impact of new measures and provisions while provide timelines for transitioning to a revised assessment system.

Preparing for English Language Proficiency Testing

State ELP testing occurs on an annual basis within a preset window that impacts all K–12 ELs in a school system. Each state is responsible for crafting a uniform set of criteria, inclusive of the ELP test scores, that contribute to determining whether ELs maintain their status for the upcoming year or are 'exited' and are consequently 'monitored' for as many as four years. As the results from the state ELP test impact state Title I accountability and the status of schools, they are considered high stakes in nature.

Gearing Up for Academic Achievement Testing

Starting in grade 3, ELs, except for their first year in the U.S. when they are exempt from the state reading/English language arts test, are subject to achievement testing along with English-language proficiency testing. Achievement testing, in addition to being burdensome and frustrating for these students, is generally not a valid means of measuring ELs' conceptual knowledge and understanding. Care must be taken in interpreting the results of achievement tests as the academic performance of ELs should not be compared to that of their English-proficient peers until ELs are at the point of reaching parity with such peers.

Taking Interim Tests

Interim achievement measures, given intermittently at a school or district level, generally have the same qualities as large-scale achievement tests. As the results serve as trajectories for student performance on state tests, these measures often carry consequences for schools and classrooms, especially those with large numbers of ELs. Therefore, stakeholders should be aware that the validity of these tests for ELs is questionable at best. Whatever state guidelines have been decided as 'accommodations' for ELs for their annual state achievement tests (which, in large part, do not improve their validity) should apply to interim measures as well as daily instruction.

May, June, July

May

It's hard to believe that yet another school year has almost gone by. Luisa looks back at what Ana has accomplished and is amazed by how she has blossomed from an introverted child unaccustomed to processing and producing English to one who enthusiastically tackles multiliteracies in two languages and readily interacts with her peers.

To close out the year, Luisa readministers the **informal reading inventories (IRI)** (and other diagnostic measures in English and Spanish that were given in September to determine each student's growth in word recognition and meaning, reading strategies, and comprehension). This structured observation enables Luisa to gain a sense of Ana's, and that of the other 2nd graders', oral and silent reading performance based on graded text passages. The IRI also provides confirmatory data as to the students' reading levels in English and Spanish to help teachers pre-plan instructional groups for the upcoming year. Being immersed in biliteracy development, Ana has made tremendous strides in both her languages this year and enthusiastically engages in learning.

Measures of Student Engagement. Under Title I of ESSA, states, as part of their accountability plan, must establish long-term goals that include the percent of ELs making progress in achieving English-language proficiency by subgroup. A new provision of the legislation requires that states also incorporate nonacademic factors in their accountability systems as indicators of school quality. Lincoln School's principal is pleased that her state decided to select 'student engagement' as one of its indicators—as everyone at the school is committed to instilling a positive identity and agency in the students.

Teacher teams at the district have reviewed instruments measuring features of student engagement in upper elementary through high school (Fredricks, et al., 2011), but initially the elementary teacher teams were stumped. Eventually, they come to an agreement on adapting one of the measures they examined that includes multiple dimensions of student engagement—academic, behavioral, cognitive, and affective. However, the measure does not tap a fifth dimension that is critical to the success of Lincoln students—the role of language in learning.

For Lincoln School and its community, linguistic engagement encompasses the extent to which languages are viewed as student resources and assets; there is a match between the languages of instruction and those of the students; and there are ongoing opportunities for student to student interaction in academic situations (Gottlieb & Castro, 2017). In the end, the teachers decide on creating, validating, and using a **self-reflective checklist** on all five dimensions of student engagement that evaluates the extent to which the school is maximizing students' opportunities to participate in learning experiences.

June

It's time for Luisa, the school staff, and the principal to collectively analyze and interpret the student data gathered throughout the year. Lincoln School has deliberately built an **assessment system** with input from students, families, teachers, and school leaders. As outlined in Figure 3, there are five levels of implementation—classroom, school, program, district, and state—each with distinct assessment measures that together constitute the system.

Balanced Assessment Across Levels of Implementation. As shown in Figure 3, the assessment system is represented as in inverted triangle for a reason—classroom data are most sensitive to students' daily accomplishments and are most authentic representations of teaching and learning. Based on Ana's story, we hope that you have come to reimagine students and teachers as partners and decision-makers in the assessment process who can make a difference in their craft. Their everyday data-driven contributions are of utmost importance and deserving of being placed atop the upturned pyramid.

The following illustrates how different types of assessment associated with each level of implementation complement each other in their purposes and uses to yield a comprehensive

FIGURE 3: Levels of Implementation of Distinct Assessment Measures

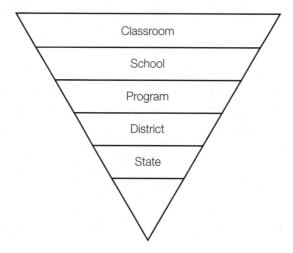

portrait of school. Although it appears that the types of assessment neatly fit into these five categories, in actuality they are interwoven, interdependent, and often occur simultaneously. Highlights of assessment for multilingual students participating in dual-language education that we have witnessed this school year include:

Classroom

- Instructional assessment or assessment *for* learning in two languages that is unique to individual teachers and their students
- Student self- and peer assessment or assessment *as* learning in two languages that promotes student agency and metalinguistic awareness

School

- Common assessment in English (and Spanish, if dual language is schoolwide) designed by teacher teams, often performance-based, with consideration for principles of Universal Design for Learning as well as linguistic and cultural sustainability
- Measures related to schoolwide initiatives, such as for grants, funded projects, or special programs

Program

- Common assessment designed for specific subgroups of students, including ELs, ELs with disabilities, and students with interrupted formal education (SIFE) to measure language development in English and Spanish
- Standardized achievement measures in Spanish

District

- Interim assessment in multiple languages; commercially produced and purchased measures, such as on-line achievement tests in reading/English language arts and mathematics
- A measure of student engagement applicable to multiple languages

State

- Screening for potential ELs
- Annual language proficiency testing (K–12) for ELs
- Achievement testing (grades 3–12) for federal (Title I) and state accountability in English
- Measurement of a nonacademic indicator

The assessment system at Lincoln School starts with students in individual classrooms and moves to the entire K–12 student population in the state. What happens day-to-day yields rich meaningful data on which teachers make thousands of instructional decisions for individual students and their classes as a whole. The primary purpose of instructional assessment is to advance student learning and improve teaching. That's what school is all about. What happens at the state level on an annual basis yields data that provide an overall index of student performance; its purpose is tied to accountability for schooling. All data sources, from classrooms to the state and all those in between, are necessary and provide insight into the functioning of schools.

During the school year, the 2nd graders and their teachers have become acclimated to a myriad of different types of assessment. Luisa has been careful to point out to her students the importance of performing their best in two languages. She is adamant about not relying on translations of measures as each language has its own linguistic and cultural nuances that are to be respected. In promoting linguistic and cultural sustainability in her classroom and around the school, Luisa has worked hard to ensure that both Spanish and English are perceived as having equal status.

July

The summer is time for continued, more extensive professional learning for Lincoln School that is part of the sustained effort that the faculty has agreed upon in their three-year plan. During the school year, there is protected time set aside each day for teachers to collaborate in co-planning and, often, co-teaching. Additionally, Luisa attends weekly meetings as a member of a professional learning community that is supported by school leadership; here she and other teachers grapple over schoolwide issues and offer recommendations to the principal. But it is during the summer that teachers and school leaders have opportunities to strengthen their **assessment literacy**. As student performance on various state tests has increasingly contributed to the determination of school ranking, teachers need to understand basic principles of both large-scale and instructional assessment and how the data from these measures can help fortify their practice.

Assessment Literacy. On one hand, assessment literacy encompasses the careful analysis of grade-level data from the score reports of statewide measures and the disaggregation of data by student subgroups. However, assessment-literate educators need to know more than the statistics displayed in the pages of a technical test manual. Additionally, teachers have to have assessment expertise that applies to their classrooms in order to maximize student learning. Luisa spends time learning how to couple instructional assessment data that she has personally collected with aggregated data from common grade-level assessment in Spanish and English with that of the total school.

Divided into their grade-level teams, teachers graph assessment results to examine trends, decide on upcoming priorities, and help group students for the upcoming year. They share their findings with the prior and next grades to ensure continuity in the spiraling of curriculum, assessment, and instruction. In addition, each team takes care in contextualizing their findings in light of student characteristics that potentially impact learning. Care is given in interpreting data for those students who have: a.) come from multilingual homes; b.) identified learning disabilities (and have Individualized Education Programs or 504 plans); c.) high rates of mobility or high rates of absenteeism; d.) witnessed or undergone trauma; e.) returned to their countries of origin one or more times; or f.) economic diversity.

According to ESSA, states and districts must report the number and percentage of ELs who are receiving language support and those who are making progress toward achieving English language proficiency in the aggregate as well as disaggregated at a minimum by ELs with disabilities. Lincoln School and many schools in the district, however, go beyond that minimum. Luisa and her colleagues and school leaders take stock of the value of the dual-language education program and acknowledge how the data they have gathered from multiple sources and in multiple languages have contributed to defining the effectiveness of the school.

Fourth Quarter Summary of Assessment and Its Extension to Other School Contexts

We have come to the end of the year for Lincoln School. Although this narrative has centered around Ana, a young girl from a Spanish-speaking country who is immersed in her inaugural year in a U.S. school, and her teacher, we hope that you have been able to apply some of their assessment experiences to your students and to yourself. The summaries have extended assessment principles and practices introduced in a three-month span to the broader K–12 audience. While there is special attention on ELs at these junctures, we hope that you can use much of this information in whatever setting you teach.

Balancing Assessment

A balanced assessment system consists of multiple measures with data gathered over time that are interpreted as a body of work. It is also one that represents varying perspectives of multiple stakeholders. Integral to the assessment system is having students and teachers assume a more substantial role in data gathering and decision making.

Whenever ELs are part of the equation, there must also be a balance in measuring language proficiency and academic achievement; these two constructs are constantly working together to better explain EL performance. In addition, if ELs are being taught in English and another language, then the notion of balance for assessment extends to the proportion of time that is devoted to each language of instruction.

Considering Student Engagement

Student engagement is one of the nonacademic factors that may be selected by states as part of their ESSA plans. It encompasses the willingness, desire, and perseverance of students in participating in and succeeding in learning. It is most prominent in classrooms where student-directed learning dominates; here is where students have opportunities to partner to create models and pose solutions to problems or work in small groups to discuss issues or plan projects. In other words, engaged students, facilitated by teachers, are actively involved in classroom activities and have a say in their academic destiny.

For ELs, having opportunities to engage in learning is critical to their social, language, and academic development. In essence, student engagement is a byproduct of a school's and classroom's culture. In schools where ELs' languages, cultures, families, and communities are welcomed and embraced, students will more likely be socially accepted, connected to curriculum, and motivated to learn.

Becoming Assessment Literate

Having educators become well versed in the principles of quality assessment and apply them to their daily contexts is an evolving process. Over the years, trends in educational assessment ebb and flow from imposing strict rigidity of high-stakes standardized tests with heavy weighting of scores to honoring the flexibility of instructional assessment by teachers and students. Consequently, teachers and school leaders must be adaptable and understand the value of the compendium of assessment tools along with how to analyze quantitative and qualitative data from which to draw inferences to better support teaching and learning that is equitable.

Assessment is more complex when ELs are involved. These uniquely heterogeneous students, such as Ana, may have strong conceptual knowledge in their home languages but simply do not yet know enough English to express themselves effectively. The issue is exacerbated when test developers and psychometricians do not consider the impact of language in the design of their measures, the analyses of data, and the interpretation of the results. Assessment literacy encompasses consideration of and input from students for whom English is an additional language, students of other varieties of English, and students, including ELs, with learning disabilities. When educators become more assessment literate and move beyond test scores to better understand the performance of their historically marginalized student populations, then assessment itself can become more equitable.

ASCD | arias®

ENCORE

THE YEAR IN REVIEW

Ana's journey from her arrival to a U.S. school in August throughout the academic year illustrates the important role of assessment with its multiple measures and the data it generates for multilingual learners who participate in dual-language education. Luisa and her team have been intentional in planning assessment month-by-month for specific purposes with comprehensive coverage of content and its related academic language use. What emerges is an understanding of the full repertoire of the students' skills and accomplishments.

We have also watched Luisa, an exceptionally dedicated bilingual teacher, navigate the languages and cultures of her classroom to optimize learning opportunities for all her students in English and in Spanish. She has promoted the interaction of students with specific outcomes in mind and has valued her students as decision makers. Consequently, her 2nd graders have gained rich experiences, identity, comfort, pride, confidence, and independence in pursuing and demonstrating learning in two languages.

Ana serves as a poster child for the empirical research that has established bilingualism and biliteracy as being cognitively, linguistically, and psychologically beneficial. For her, the development of biliteracy has meant doubling her assets and extending her conceptual insights within and across two languages. Indeed, the value of Ana's participation in a dual-language classroom and seeing her flourish, as evidenced from multiple data sources, is an outcome of which we can all be proud.

Assessment takes on various forms that are reflective of specific purposes and uses of data. It is ever-present in our classrooms today and it is foundational to knowing where students are academically and linguistically in relation to where they need to go next. A shared knowledge base between teachers and students, along with a common vision and direction, must be part of this journey. When classrooms are linguistically and culturally sustainable places to collaborate, co-construct meaning, and are places where all students learn together, ELs, their peers, and teachers thrive.

References

Every Student Succeeds Act of 2015, Pub. L. No. 114-95 § 114 Stat. 1177 (2015–2016).

Fredricks, J., McColskey, W., Meli, J., Mordica, J., Montrosse, B., and Mooney, K. (2011). *Measuring student engagement in upper elementary through high school: a description of 21 instruments.* (Issues & Answers Report, REL 2011–No. 098). Washington, DC: U.S. Department of Education, Institute of Education Sciences, National Center for Education Evaluation and Regional Assistance, Regional Educational Laboratory Southeast. Retrieved from http://ies.ed.gov/ncee/edlabs

Gottlieb, M. (2016). *Assessing English language learners: Bridges to educational equity: Connecting academic language proficiency to student achievement* (2nd Ed.). Thousand Oaks, CA: Corwin.

Gottlieb, M., & Castro, M. (2017). *Language power: Key uses for accessing content.* Thousand Oaks, CA: Corwin.

Gottlieb, M., & Ernst Slavit, G. (2014). *Academic language in diverse classrooms: Definitions and contexts.* Thousand Oaks, CA: Corwin.

Vygotsky, L. S. (1978). *Mind in society: The development of higher psychological processes.* Cambridge, MA: Harvard University Press.

WIDA. (2016). *Los descriptores Podemos: Usos clave del lenguaje académico en español. 2.º y 3.º grados.* Junta de Regentes del Sistema de la Universidad de Wisconsin, en representación de WIDA.

WIDA. (2016). Board of Regents of the University of Wisconsin System, on behalf of WIDA. The *WIDA Can Do Descriptors, Key Uses Edition, Grades 2–3.* Board of Regents of the University of Wisconsin System, on behalf of the WIDA Consortium. www.wida.us

Wiggins, G., & McTighe, J. (2005). *Understanding by design* (2nd Ed.). Alexandria, VA: ASCD.

Related ASCD Resources

At the time of publication, the following ASCD resources were available (ASCD stock numbers appear in parentheses). For up-to-date information about ASCD resources, go to www.ascd.org. You can search the complete archives of *Educational Leadership* at http://www.ascd.org/el.

ASCD EDge® Group
Exchange ideas and connect with other educators on the social networking site ASCD EDge at http://ascdedge.ascd.org/.

Print Products
Educational Leadership: Culturally Diverse Classrooms (March 2015) (#115021)

Educational Leadership: Helping ELLs Excel (February 2016) (#116032)

Educating Everybody's Children: Diverse Teaching Strategies for Diverse Learners, Revised and Expanded 2nd Edition by Robert W. Cole (#100210)

The Language-Rich Classroom: A Research-Based Framework for Teaching English Language Learners by Pérsida Himmele & William Himmele (#107003)

Classroom Instruction That Works with English Language Learners, 2nd Edition by Jane D. Hill & Kirsten B. Miller (#114004)

Getting Started with English Language Learners: How Educators Can Meet the Challenge by Judie Haynes (#106048)

Teaching English Language Learners Across the Content Areas by Judie Haynes and Debbie Zacarian (#109032)

For more information, send e-mail to member@ascd.org; call 1-800-933-2723 or 703-578-9600; send a fax to 703-575-5400; or write to Information Services, ASCD, 1703 N. Beauregard St., Alexandria, VA 22311-1714 USA.

About the Author

Margo Gottlieb is co-founder and lead developer for WIDA at the Wisconsin Center for Education Research, University of Wisconsin-Madison, and former director, assessment and evaluation, Illinois Resource Center. Margo, who began her career as an ESL and bilingual teacher, has worked with schools, school districts, states, governments, and universities. Over the last decade, she has focused on creating English-language proficiency/development standards for multiple entities, designing student-centered assessment systems, and crafting comprehensive curricular frameworks around academic language use.

Gottlieb, a Fulbright Senior Specialist in Chile and appointed to the U.S. Department of Education's Inaugural National Technical Advisory Council, was honored by TESOL International Association in 2016 "as an individual who has made a significant contribution to the TESOL profession within the past 50 years." She has presented in 19 countries and 44 states. Her publications include more than 80 articles, monographs, handbooks, and book chapters. Additionally, she has authored and coauthored several books on language proficiency standards, academic language in diverse class-rooms, assessment and accountability, common language assessment, and assessment of English-language learners. Her most recent book, coauthored with M. Castro, is *Language Power: Key uses for accessing content* (Corwin, 2017). You are welcome to contact Margo at margogottlieb@gmail.com.

WHAT KEEPS YOU UP AT NIGHT?

ASCD Arias provide the answers you need today—in a convenient format you can read in one sitting and immediately put into practice. Available in both print and digital editions.

Answers You Need
from Voices You Trust

ASCD | arias™

For more information, go to www.ascdarias.org or call (toll-free in the United States and Canada) 800-933-ASCD (2723).

www.ascdarias.org